EXPLORING OUR OCEANS

ATLANTIC OCEAN

by Avery Toolen

pogo

Ideas for Parents and Teachers

Pogo Books let children practice reading informational text while introducing them to nonfiction features such as headings, labels, sidebars, maps, and diagrams, as well as a table of contents, glossary, and index.

Carefully leveled text with a strong photo match offers early fluent readers the support they need to succeed.

Before Reading

- "Walk" through the book and point out the various nonfiction features. Ask the student what purpose each feature serves.
- Look at the glossary together. Read and discuss the words.

Read the Book

- Have the child read the book independently.
- Invite him or her to list questions that arise from reading.

After Reading

- Discuss the child's questions. Talk about how he or she might find answers to those questions.
- Prompt the child to think more. Ask: Overfishing is an issue in the Atlantic Ocean. How do you think this affects the ocean's food web?

Pogo Books are published by Jump!
5357 Penn Avenue South
Minneapolis, MN 55419
www.jumplibrary.com

Library of Congress Cataloging-in-Publication Data

Names: Toolen, Avery, author.
Title: Atlantic Ocean / by Avery Toolen.
Description: Minneapolis, MN: Jump!, Inc., 2023.
Series: Exploring our oceans | Includes index.
Audience: Ages 7-10
Identifiers: LCCN 2021051352 (print)
LCCN 2021051353 (ebook)
ISBN 9781636907710 (hardcover)
ISBN 9781636907727 (paperback)
ISBN 9781636907734 (ebook)
Subjects: LCSH: Atlantic Ocean–Juvenile literature.
Classification: LCC GC481 .T66 2023 (print)
LCC GC481 (ebook) | DDC 910.9163–dc23
LC record available at
https://lccn.loc.gov/2021051352
LC ebook record available at
https://lccn.loc.gov/2021051353

Editor: Jenna Gleisner
Designer: Emma Bersie

Photo Credits: Gonzalo Jara/Shutterstock, cover (dolphin); HillebrandBreuker/Shutterstock, cover (puffin); Michael Bogner/Shutterstock, 1; Lewis Burnett/Shutterstock, 3; Harvepino/Shutterstock, 4; one pony/Shutterstock, 5; Vyacheslav Lopatin/Alamy, 6-7; Drew McArthur/Shutterstock, 8-9; Artem Gorlanov/Shutterstock, 10-11; Damsea/Shutterstock, 12; Jeremy Richards/Shutterstock, 13; Gabriel Rojo/Alamy, 14-15; Mayskyphoto/Shutterstock, 16; Xavier DESMIER/Getty, 17; Marcus Bay/Shutterstock, 18-19; Love Lego/Shutterstock, 20-21; Ciprian23/Shutterstock, 23.

Printed in the United States of America at Corporate Graphics in North Mankato, Minnesota.

TABLE OF CONTENTS

CHAPTER 1

NORTH AND SOUTH

The Atlantic Ocean is big. It covers about 20 percent of Earth's **surface**! Of Earth's five oceans, it is the second largest.

It is made up of salt water. In the Caribbean Sea, the water temperature can be 84 degrees Fahrenheit (29 degrees Celsius). Near Canada, it can get below freezing. Ice forms!

The ocean is split into two areas. They are the North Atlantic and South Atlantic. They have different **currents**.

The Gulf Stream is in the North Atlantic. This warm current flows across the Atlantic from North America toward Europe and Africa. It warms land near the water.

TAKE A LOOK!

Where is the Atlantic Ocean? Take a look!

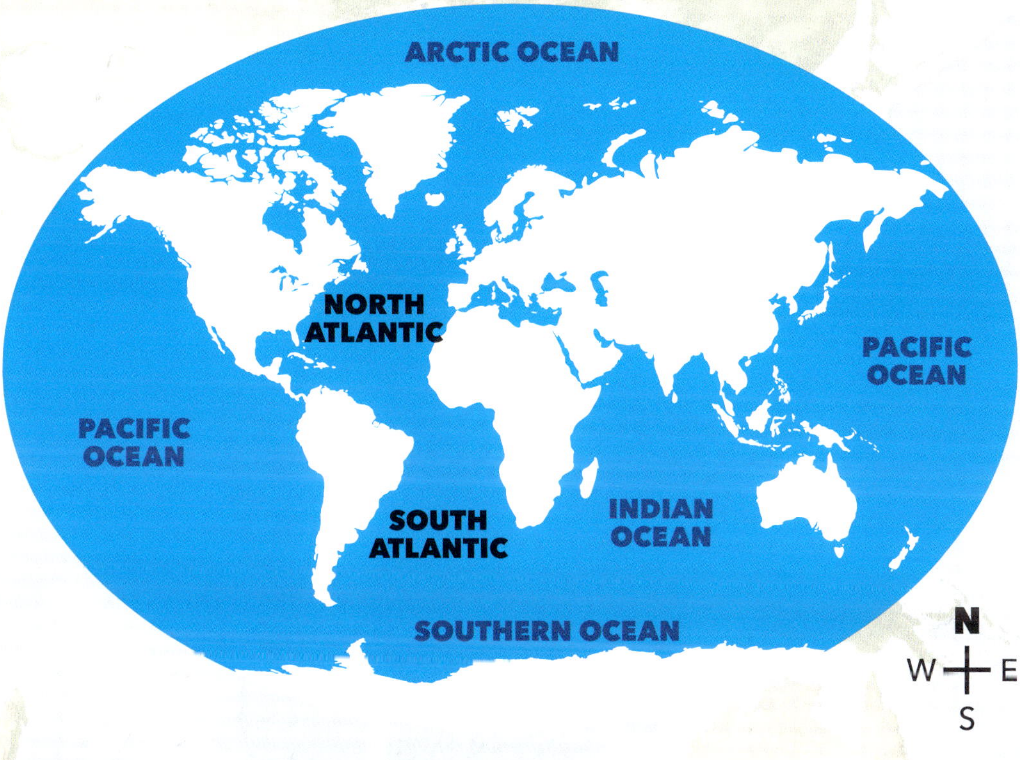

Hurricanes are common. These storms form above warm water near the **equator**. They gain strength from warm air and water. They most often hit land in the Caribbean and southeastern United States. They bring high winds, rain, and flooding.

The Mid-Atlantic Ridge is in the Atlantic Ocean. This mountain range is mostly underwater. But we can see part of it in Iceland!

Two **plates** are on either side of the ridge. They are spreading apart. As they spread underwater, lava comes out of Earth's **mantle**. It can form volcanic islands.

TAKE A LOOK!

How does a volcanic island form? Take a look!

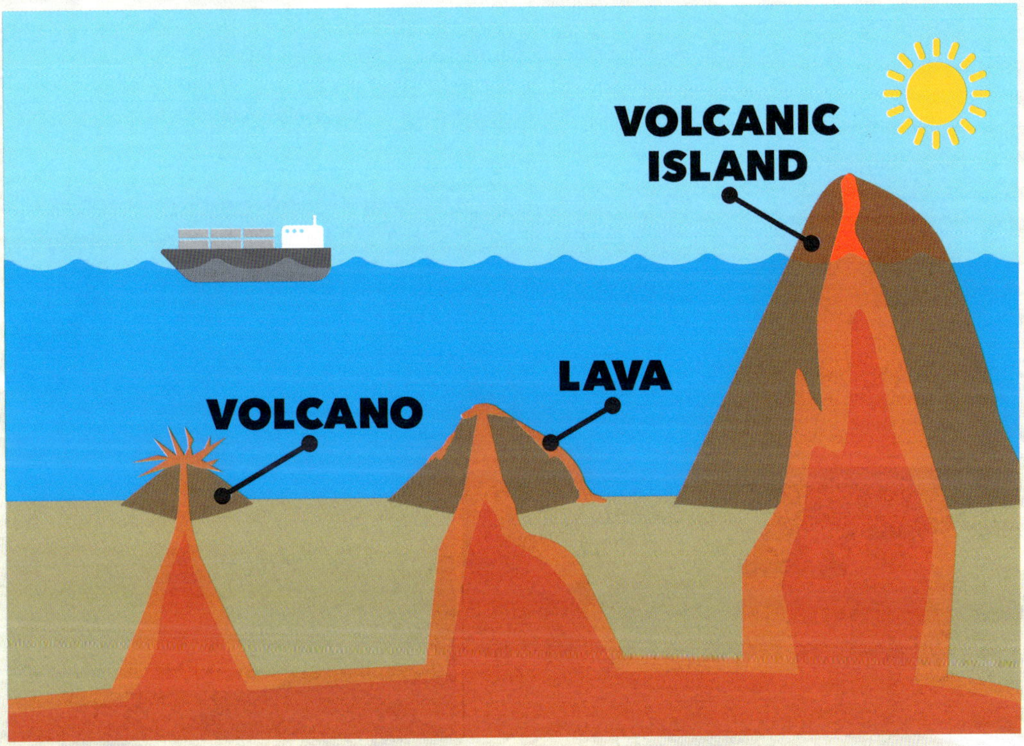

1
A volcano **erupts** on the ocean floor. Lava flows out of Earth's mantle.

2
Lava continues to flow out. It builds up over time.

3
When the lava rises above the water, it forms an island.

CHAPTER 2

ATLANTIC ANIMALS

Coral reefs in the Atlantic are home to fish, crabs, and sea stars. Sea turtles, octopuses, and more live in them, too.

Atlantic puffins spend much of their time in the open ocean. They come to shore to nest. They bring fish to their young!

Atlantic spotted dolphins are only found in this ocean. Sharks and whales swim in it, too. North Atlantic right whales are one kind.

DID YOU KNOW?

North Atlantic right whales are **endangered**. Why? People used to hunt them. Some are hit by ships.

North Atlantic right whale

CHAPTER 3

EXPLORING THE ATLANTIC

People have been exploring this ocean for thousands of years. Today, ships **trade**, travel, and fish here.

Some ships have sunk in the Atlantic. On April 14, 1912, the R.M.S. *Titanic* hit an **iceberg**. It broke in half. Then it sank 12,600 feet (3,840 meters). It still rests on the ocean floor.

R.M.S. *Titanic*

Divers explore ships that have sunk. Scientists dive to study wildlife. They visit coral reefs.

DID YOU KNOW?

Climate change is warming the oceans. **Pollution** and **overfishing** also harm ocean wildlife. Scientists study how these changes affect Earth.

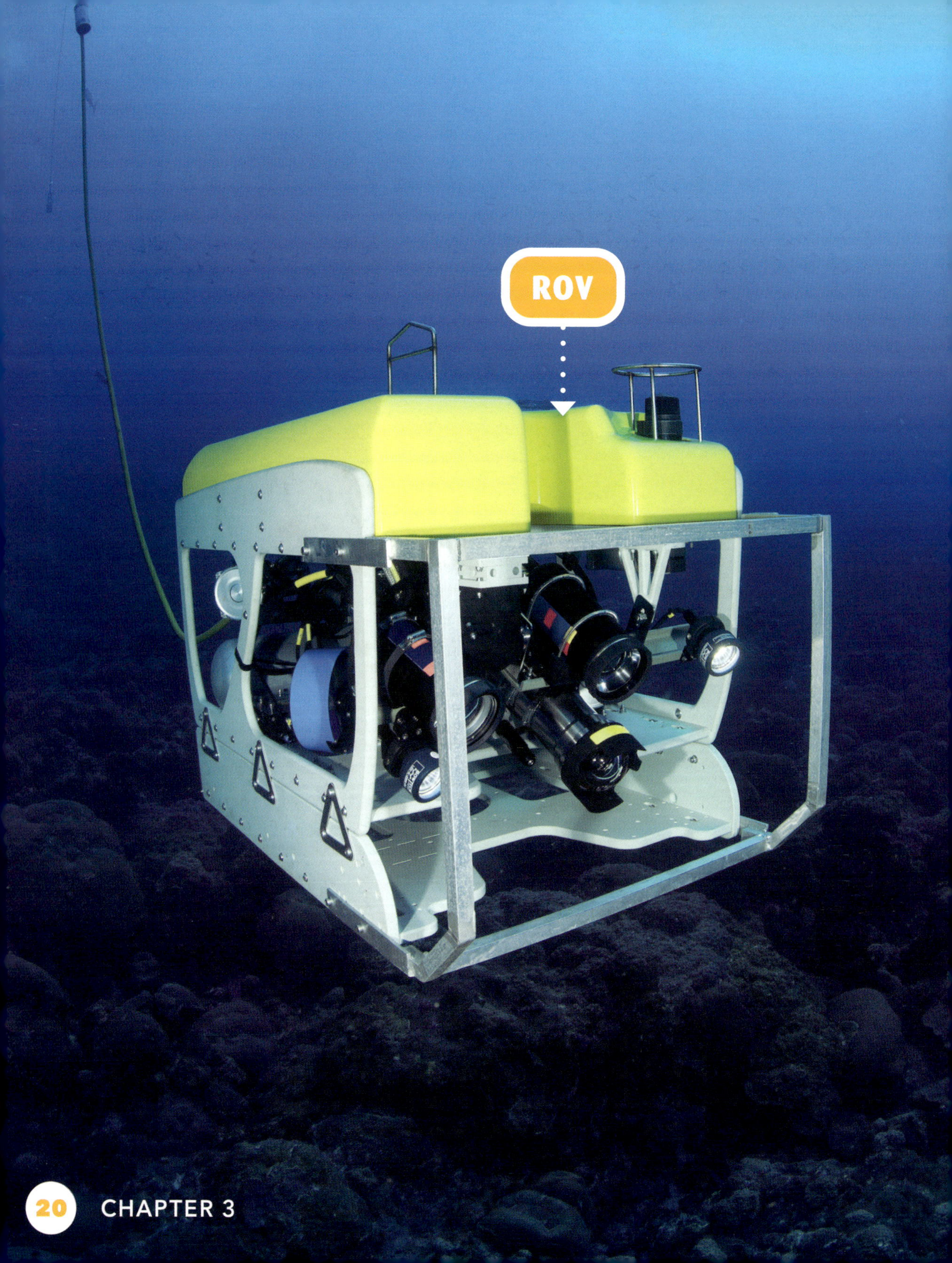
ROV

The ocean floor is often too deep for divers to explore. Scientists use remotely operated vehicles (ROVs). These map the ocean floor. They record information on deep-sea **species**. Sometimes, scientists discover new species!

Would you like to explore the Atlantic Ocean? What do you think you might find?

ACTIVITIES & TOOLS

TRY THIS!

EARTH'S PLATES

Plates make up Earth's crust.
Underneath is the mantle.
This is where lava flows from.
See how it works with this fun activity!

What You Need:

- plate or flat dish
- whipped cream
- butter knife
- graham crackers

1. Spread whipped cream onto a plate. Your layer of whipped cream should be about one centimeter deep. Use a butter knife to smooth the surface. The whipped cream is your mantle layer.
2. Place two graham crackers beside one another on top of the whipped cream. The crackers are Earth's plates.
3. Gently push down on the graham crackers while pulling them apart toward the sides of the plate.
4. What happens to the mantle? How do you think this is similar to what is happening along the Mid-Atlantic Ridge?

GLOSSARY

climate change: Changes in Earth's weather and climate over time.

coral reefs: Long lines of coral that lie in warm, shallow waters.

currents: Movements of water in one direction.

endangered: In danger of becoming extinct, usually because of human activity.

equator: An imaginary line around the middle of Earth that is an equal distance from the North and South Poles.

erupts: Suddenly throws out lava, hot ashes, and steam.

iceberg: A large mass of ice that breaks off from a glacier and floats in the sea.

mantle: The part of Earth, between the crust and the core, where lava comes from.

overfishing: Catching too many fish so there are not enough remaining.

plates: Flat, rigid, rocky pieces that make up Earth's outer crust.

pollution: Harmful materials that damage or contaminate the air, water, and soil.

species: One of the groups into which similar animals and plants are divided.

surface: The outermost layer of something.

trade: To buy and sell goods.

INDEX

TO LEARN MORE

Finding more information is as easy as 1, 2, 3.

1. Go to www.factsurfer.com
2. Enter "AtlanticOcean" into the search box.
3. Choose your book to see a list of websites.

FACT SURFER